Should I Quit My Job?:
How to Cope with a Dead End Job, Explore All Options Before Quitting Your Job

Table of Contents

Introduction

We all know that a job can provide money and career prospects, but with that comes pressure, tension, and expectations from the work environment. Oftentimes, people take that drama home with them, and let it affect every aspect of their lives. Life would surely be much easier if we could just quit our jobs and leave those miserable workplaces. But, in reality, most of us have responsibilities and a pile of bills to pay, so the idea of quitting just isn't an option. Quitting a job without planning can negatively impact your career and disrupt your personal life. However, staying in an undesirable situation for too long can be even worse.

In the following chapters, I will be sharing a lot of important advice on preparing to resign from a job, and I will provide you with you different ways of minimizing risk, so that you can cope while planning of quitting your dead end job.

There are many reasons people give for resigning from their positions. Not all of these are legitimate, but they are among the most common reasons provided by people who quit their jobs.

Stress, being overworked, and having an unhealthy working environment are among the many valid reasons given for quitting. These, however, are psychological problems which arise from other workplace issues that may not have been addressed by the employer or company.

Other reasons for resignation include limited growth opportunities and the need for change. These might be some of your reasons for quitting if you have a temp job, or a job which provides little opportunity for professional growth. The job might not provide enough challenge, so you want to find a better position elsewhere.

Additionally, some employees are forced to leave their jobs as a result of company downsizing or mergers that have caused their positions to be dissolved.

Risk management is very important if you are on the verge of quitting your job, you cannot do so without fully justifying your decision to your employers. You also need to make preparations.

Quitting your job should never be a spur-of-the-moment decision, since you could find yourself in dire straits if you quit without giving proper notice, and without a backup plan. Before you hand in that resignation letter, here are some things you should consider:

Can you afford to lose your job at this point? Do you have a financial nest-egg that can tide you over while you are in-between jobs? How will you be paying your bills if you lose your job? If you cannot answer these questions, it might not be the right time to quit just yet.

Is the situation hopeless? Is quitting really the only way out? Have you considered staying on and trying to change things at work? Remember, quitting your job is final and irrevocable; more often than not it is a last resort caused by unresolved issues at your workplace.

How are your work problems affecting your personal life? Sometimes, the situation demands an immediate resolution, especially if your job is already affecting your quality time with your family, and/or causing you undue stress and psychological problems. If that is the case, you really need to prepare the other aspects mentioned prior in order to leave as soon as possible.

If you are truly set on quitting your job, you must not do it in a negative way that could affect your future employment prospects. Quitting without prior notice could earn you a negative reputation that will reflect on your resumé, perhaps implicating that you were a difficult employee.

There are ways to make a graceful exit from your workplace without antagonizing your employers. You will need to utilize tact and some simple techniques to make sure your decision will result in no hard feelings for you or your employer. The world is very small, and there is a chance that you might have to come back and work for the same employer.

Chapter 1: Real Reasons For Quitting

Behind the common excuses that people use for quitting their jobs lie real and legitimate reasons that stem not from personal problems, but from issues concerning management or company policy.

The following reasons are not things you would want to write about in your resignation letter, but they are definitely excellent reasons for quitting your job.

Low pay

Not all people will admit it openly, but this is often one of the primary reasons why employees quit their jobs. Salary and compensation, after all, are the reasons why people need a job in the first place.

Being underpaid is a legitimate reason for quitting, especially if you are always saddled with a lot of work in exchange for a measly hourly wage. It's also one of the top reasons why people seek greener pastures elsewhere, somewhere the same workload will get them better pay.

Under-compensation goes hand-in-hand with feeling undervalued, which could in turn lead to a form of personal crisis. When you feel you are not being adequately rewarded for your efforts, you begin to question your worth to the company and whether or not you deserve such shabby treatment.

This can be particularly frustrating if you've been with the company for years. If you feel that you are being paid less than what you deserve, especially after being such a loyal employee, then your reasons for quitting are fully justified.

It's normal to ask for recognition and praise, both in terms of monetary compensation and morale-boosting. When you don't get both (or either) of those things, it only increases your dissatisfaction with your current workplace, and might snowball into bigger issues as time passes.

If this is one of the primary factors affecting your decision, it might be the right time to accept that your current job has hit a dead end. If you have been asking for promotions or better compensation, but your requests have fallen on deaf ears, it's probably time to hit the job-hunting road again.

Lack of challenge

This is actually one of the top reasons people quit their jobs: a job has become monotonous and there are no real challenges to face.

It happens when you become accustomed to the current "drill" at your workplace, and nothing new comes along. Any job opportunity should provide you with a chance to grow professionally, so if you've been a temp for a year or so with no prospect of getting promoted in sight, you begin to feel more than a little frustrated.

Remember, your job should always make you feel a bit challenged, enough so that you can find enjoyment in doing it. If this is not the case with your current job, and there are no imminent opportunities to change things within the company, you should definitely consider bailing out.

Boredom and lack of challenge may sound like personal problems, but often, there is an issue with company policy as well. It's normal to seek professional growth and development, particularly if you are set on a career that you love.

So, if you've been feeling this lack of challenge for some time, you should probably notify your employer and see what can be done —i.e., ascertain whether a promotion or a change of position is possible.

However, if you have already done all that you can and you still feel the issue of adequate challenge is unresolved, it's time to move on, before things take a turn for the worst. If left unaddressed, boredom can result in bigger problems, to the point where you no longer enjoy your work and end up hitting a midlife crisis.

Stress and depression are serious psychological problems that could eventually result from job dissatisfaction. So, if you're no longer happy with your work or you feel bored and think you deserve something better, don't be afraid to let go instead of holding on to a job that no longer works for you.

No enjoyment

The last, but no less real, reason people quit their jobs is because they are no longer happy with their current job. A number of factors can cause this predicament:

Work-life imbalance. When a job becomes so demanding that it takes away your personal quality time, or when you find yourself taking your work home, it can result in being overworked and stressed. You are challenged to the brink of a breaking point, which can be very unhealthy for many people.

Lack of security. Stress can result from your current position being unstable, or if the company you work for has been hit by the difficult economic situation and layoffs are being made. You cannot be happy if you are constantly worrying about losing your job.

General dissatisfaction. Menial jobs tend to become wearing as time passes. Even when there is adequate compensation, if the job isn't really something you enjoy doing, it becomes more of a burden just to get ready for work in the morning.

Workplace issues. An overly competitive atmosphere with your colleagues, and lack of support from management, can quickly lead to an unhealthy working relationship with your peers.

Having a healthy working environment is vital to increasing your productivity, but if you cannot find that at your current workplace, it can lead to personal dissatisfaction.

These are only some of the reasons you might not find your work as enjoyable as you once did. If you feel you can no longer find happiness with your current employer, then it would probably the best for both of you, and the company, if you hand in your resignation now.

Staying on when you no longer feel satisfied can only be destructive—both for your personal welfare and the company's productivity levels. It's best to resign early rather than do it too late.

So, if you have decided to quit, you need to prepare yourself while waiting for the right time to hand in your resignation. Make sure you clear out your desk and leave no loose ends hanging. Draft your resignation letter ahead of time, keeping it brief and simple — you don't need to explain your decision extensively.

If you're still unsure, however, and you feel you need time to think, you definitely have options you can act on while still deciding. These steps should help you figure out what the final step you should take is.

Chapter 2: You Have Options

Employees should never be made to feel like they've come to a forced end with their current job, one where the only solution to their problems is quitting. However, when the inevitable happens, you should be able to take one of several options to remedy matters.

The first step you should take is to stop feeling down about your situation. Analyze the hard facts before you take the final step — that is, deciding between quitting your job or staying on, trying to mend things. Here are some things you can do to clear your head enough to decide:

Go part-time

If lack of challenge is the most pressing problem with your job, you could try going part-time, if possible, so you'll have the time to go looking for another job.

This will be your 'trial period' in which you can test other jobs and see if that makes a difference in how you feel. It can also help you make comparisons between your current job and other jobs.

Trying other jobs can also help you put your current job in perspective. It can give you an idea of what you will be facing if you decide to quit your job altogether. It can also give you an insight on what's missing from your current job, so you can discuss your concerns with your employer.

It's crucial, however, that you don't overwork yourself with different jobs. Make sure you can handle the pressure and demands of having several jobs at a time. It won't be beneficial for you if your job performance drops simply because you've taken on too much work. In fact, it can lead to stress and overload if you don't watch it.

Vacation time

Sometimes, all you need is a break to clear your head, particularly if you are feeling overworked or depressed. When you're not yet sure whether quitting is the best decision or whether there are other options, you can take some leave and get your well-deserved break.

Use this time to consider your options, and to relax and unwind from all the work-related stress you've accumulated over the time you've been working your head off. You can spend more quality time with your family, or you can choose to take a trip somewhere.

Vacations are a great way to regain your zeal and strength, since too much work can lead to emotional and psychological problems. They are also perfect when you need to distance yourself from your work in order to examine your situation objectively.

Make the most of your vacation. It's the best time to list all the pros and cons of quitting your job, and your immediate concerns should you decide to quit. It's also the time to conceive backup plans, and to start looking for alternate jobs that you can apply for before giving up your current job.

If you're thinking of staying on, then use your vacation to fix your mindset. Make a list of the good things about your work and the things that could be improved. If you want to improve your situation, you can list suggested changes that you can later discuss with your employer, once you get back.

Either way, going on vacation will definitely buy you some time before you make any irrevocable decisions that will change your career forever.

Discuss professionally with your boss

The best approach to take when you feel dissatisfied with your current job is to discuss politely with your immediate superior. That way, you are informing your employer that you value their opinions, and it shows that you want to work things out with them.

Now, it could prove problematic if one of your concerns is actually your working relationship with your boss. If that is the case, you should approach the human relations department of the company to address your concerns. If you feel you have been treated unfairly, now is the time to air your grievances — but only through the proper channel.

Before you approach your superiors to renegotiate your current position, make sure you do the following:

Make a list of your concerns. This can serve as your guide when you are on the negotiation table, so you can avoid veering off-topic and engaging in heated arguments.

Along with your concerns, make a list of demands and suggestions for change. However, remember that when you are angling for a promotion or pay raise, you are entering a flexible negotiation process. You should provide enough elbow room for the management to make their counter-offers.

If you are having emotional or psychological problems such as stress, work overload, or depression, it's best if you seek the help of an expert on how to handle the negotiations. This will help you avoid emotional outbursts which could be counter-productive to the purpose of you meeting with your bosses.

During negotiations, keep a cool head and stick to the facts. Avoid making unfounded accusations or emotionally loaded statements. That way, you get to the heart of the matter immediately and see if your case has a chance of being resolved within the company or not.

Quitting your job should never be voiced as a threat to management. Remember, no individual member of the company is truly indispensable, and there will be hundreds of applicants lining up to take your place.

Quitting should only be broached as a last resort if things truly don't work out for you, or if the management fails to put your concerns into perspective and address them.

Having an employer who is insensitive to your needs is the worst experience for any good employee. If you have taken all these options and still the management ignores your concerns, then the situation is out of your hands. It's time to get out while you still can and maintain your dignity.

When you hit that final snag, it's time to put your backup plans into action. You should now plan your graceful exit from the company and rely on alternate means to tide yourself over as you search for the new career path ahead of you.

Chase after your passion

Perhaps you are burnt out because you feel like you have dedicated your whole life to your job, which you may now feel was not really worth it at all. Due to your demanding job, you have probably given up your personal and social life. Well, it is about time that you reconnect.

Work is indeed necessary to earn a living, but your life should not revolve around it entirely. Whether you are in your 20s, 30s, 40s, 50s, or even older, it is never too late to chase after your passion. Take Colonel Harland Sanders, for example. He was already a senior citizen living on his pension when he decided to introduce his original fried chicken recipe to the rest of the world. He eventually pulled it off, and now KFC is one of the most successful fast food restaurant chains in the world.

Have you always wanted to do something but your commitment to your job held you back?

Have you always wanted to go on a trip but your schedule won't allow it?

Is there a hobby you have always wanted to explore but you never seem to have time?

Have you been missing out on family events or hanging out with your friends?

Whatever it is that you have in mind or whether you have a list or not, just remember that catchphrase from that famous shoe brand: "Just do it!" Now that you have the luxury of time, go run after your passion and start living outside of your job. Treat this time as a breather from the stress that the corporate world brings. Its time to be free and do what you have always wanted, implement what you planned, on and know what it feels like to live free!

Start a business

There are basically two types of people. There are the thinkers who are great at planning and yet never seem to move forward because they do nothing but plan. On the other hand, there are the doers. They may not be as good in planning but their biggest advantage over thinkers is that they take action.

Are you a thinker or a doer? A lot of people dream about putting up a business but they also fear the uncertainty of such a venture. From an employee's point of view, your job could have been holding you back all this time to take action. Now, you do not have any excuse. You can either start looking for another employer or you can become your own boss in your own business.

Do you have a business idea in mind?

What is it that you feel passionate about?

What are you good at?

How much money do you have prepared for the investment?

Perhaps these questions seem overwhelming, but look on the bright side; it is an exciting time for you. To get you started, below are some business ideas you may want to consider. The good thing about these businesses is that they require low startup capital.

Online retailing

Think about what you can sell that you are genuinely interested in. Start with a few basic products and build your inventory gradually. You do not even have to put up your own website immediately. You can use eBay and other e-retailing sites in the meantime.

Online English Tutoring

All you need is Skype, a website, and a bank account. Because of globalization, non-English speaking countries are pressured to cope. That provides a low-cost business opportunity for you.

Wellness instructor

Obesity and simply being overweight are still huge problems which is why the fitness business is projected to increase by 29% by 2018. If you have a background in health and fitness, you can help other people get in shape.

You do not necessarily have to invest in gym equipment. Rather, hold classes in the local gym or in the park. Offer boot camps and start marketing your services online. Acquiring a certification will give you more credibility in the eyes of your intended market.

Party planning

Events and reasons for celebration never run out. If you have a penchant for planning, then you may just be able to pull this off. In this case, you must leverage your network in order to land a gig. It will help if you have managed to build your network from your previous job.

Personal chef or Home catering business

This is a fast-growing industry, having reached $1.2 billion in 2010 alone. This is perfect if you have a passion for cooking or have a background in this kind of work. You can rent equipment first and start investing gradually as you earn.

Tour guide operator

If you like socialize with people or you are particularly living in a place that attracts tourists, this is a good business idea for you. The key is to find your niche. For instance, if you are physically active, then you can promote a biking tour. On the other hand, if you are an art enthusiast, you can conduct a tour through local museums and galleries.

Whatever business idea you choose to pursue, plan it well and do not forget to take action!

Continuing Education

Life is a constant learning experience. If you feel like you have taken a wrong turn in the choice of a career, know that it is never too late to start over again. There are a number of online courses available now so you do not necessarily have to live as you did back in college. The schedules are more flexible so you can take classes on your own time.

Start by reassessing your new career options. Think about your passion, what it is that you like doing, and what it is you can actually do. Once you have figured those out, the search will be easy.

Most people who find themselves out of work choose to become bums in the meantime. You can do that but you can also make use of this time to take charge of your future. Plan your transition and have a better shot at life.

Chapter 3: Planning For The Exit

Before you quit your job (assuming that you have finally decided to make that decision), there are several things that you should prepare for. It's never wise to quit a job when you have no immediate plans on how you will survive after leaving your job.

Practically speaking, financial security is your primary concern. Only people who are financially secure can afford to quit at a moment's notice. For most people, it's difficult to give up a job no matter how paltry the pay is or how crappy the working conditions are, simply because they have no backup plans for the future.

You don't need to make a lot of fuss with your resignation. There is a way to ensure you have a graceful exit, without any bitter feelings on both parties. Here are some tips if you want to be able to make a clean break from your current job:

Budgeting

Whether or not you are planning to quit your job in the future, saving up a portion of your pay is a great way to ensure your financial security in case you fall on hard times. That way, you are slowly building up your nest egg, a form of savings you could dip into when your source of income becomes unstable.

Saving for the future isn't so difficult, and you could achieve it by carefully allocating your earnings around your expenses. Here are some quick tips on how you can save more of your earnings:

- Learn to live within your means and avoid unnecessary spending.

- Use your credit cards sparingly, and set a fixed portion of your daily wage as automatic savings.

- Pay off your debts consistently to avoid bigger interests, and avoid incurring new ones.

- Before purchasing anything, ask yourself first if this is an absolutely necessary item.

- If you can, get some insurance or retirement plans. Pay these regularly and you will have a sure way of keeping yourself afloat financially.

Your savings will be your emergency funds while in between jobs and you can in fact use them to look for a new job.

Have a plan to pay bills

Financial obligations are a reality for adults. If people do not have to worry about these responsibilities then nobody would care if they are out of work, but the truth is this is something you have to face in case you do decide to quit.

Among the most expensive things that need to be taken care of are house rent and vehicle fees. The last thing you would want is to end up living in the street simply because you failed to plan ahead. So, how do you exactly deal with paying basic expenses?

Taking care of the house rent

Before you hand over your resignation, make sure that you have already thought about your living situation. Your apartment or house may become too expensive when you no longer have your primary source of income, so what is it that you can do to avoid being homeless? Here are a few suggestions.

Have an idea of your monthly expenses

As I mention before, saving up is really important. How long can your savings cover your rent? Keep in mind that you have other expenses to take care of on top of rent. How much really is enough?

This is one of the biggest reasons why you always have to make calculated decisions. How much time do you need to get settled in with a new job or a new business, whatever it is that you plan to do next?

If you think that 3 months is enough time to get you covered, save up for more than 3 months. You never know what could happen in between. So, fatten up your savings before you quit.

Get a roommate

If you are living solo in your apartment, perhaps you can get a roommate. Cutting the rental expenses by half can make a big difference.

Living with someone else may not be something you are used to. However, in these times, you have to be practical. In fact, you do not have to get a total stranger for a roommate. You can ask friends of your friends.

On the other hand, if your abode is only meant for a single person, then you may want to let it go so you can move in and be a roommate in somebody else's apartment. You have to plan this ahead of time so you do not waste money and time.

Move in with your parents

Desperate times call for desperate measures. This may mean you would have to swallow your pride, but if that is what it takes for you to regain composure, then you must choose this option.

Think about it. When you move back in with your parents, you would not have to worry about rent at all. While this living situation has its share of downsides such as losing your independence, it does have its perks too, particularly in reducing your expenditures.

Talk to your parents about your plans. If they know what your future plans are, they would not worry that much. Consider this as a setback. Emphasize that it is just a temporary situation and make good on that promise!

Stay with a friend

If you have made generous and accommodating friends, then your friend can save you from the rather uncomfortable feeling of moving back in with your parents. However, do keep in mind that this is supposed to be temporary so do not get too comfortable with the arrangement.

In return for the free stay, offer your personal services. Do your share of the house chores such as cooking and cleaning. You may also offer to take care of the groceries.

As much as possible, you would not want to take advantage of a friend's generosity. Do not be too imposing. Be an adult and be a responsible even if you're just "crashing" for the meantime. Anyway, this is just an idea and you may choose to take it or leave it.

So, after quitting your job, what route do you wish to take as far as your living situation is concerned? To what extent can your savings take care of you or for how long?

This is not meant to scare you. Rather, it is a reality check. You will have to deal with this matter sooner or later, and the sooner you take care of it, the better off your will be.

Taking care of the vehicle fee

In addition to house rent, another expense you must plan ahead for has to do with owning a car. Sure, there are perks to having your own car, but when it is crunch time with your finances, you better have a backup plan. What exactly can you do with the car expense?

Sell your vehicle

You may have gotten a car for a more convenient way of traveling from your house to where you work, but if you are quitting, then you may no longer require it. It is good to keep around but just think about the expense of maintaining ownership when you do not have a primary source of income anymore.

Think about selling the car. If you are keeping it, your costs will pile up. You will have to continue paying for it if you have not yet fully paid up. Moreover, there is the cost of insurance. Your monthly premium will not freeze just because you let your job go. The expenses meter will keep running whether or not you drive your car.

Understand that there are a few things you have to let go. Consider it a necessary sacrifice so you can get by. It will not always be this way. You should not feel bitter or lose hope nor should you get too attached to it. It is just a car and you can replace it (or even buy it back if you want it that much) once you have reestablished yourself.

Take public transport

This time, you have to get used to taking public transport to get to where you need to be. Commuting is definitely cheaper than paying for gas, parking, insurance, and other vehicle-related expenses. People take the train and the bus all the time. It is not big deal.

In fact, you are doing the environment a huge favor by not contributing to pollution since you are saving fuel by not driving your own car.

Get a bike

Another option for transportation is riding a bicycle. A bike is not high-maintenance like the car you own. It does not require fuel – only your good strong legs. Biking can also help you stay in shape without even paying for gym membership!

Other money-saving ideas

The point is when it comes to letting some of your valuables go, it is important that you recognize the bright side of things. Otherwise, you will never consider quitting even if it means enduring a job that you are no longer happy about. That said, below are a few more ideas on how you can stay financially afloat after quitting your job.

Downgrade your cell phone plan

If you are signed up for a particularly expensive plan, it is time to downgrade. Ask your provider for a cheaper plan. Make sure to get your calculations right and get a plan that you can afford. Giving up your data plan is definitely worth it since there are so many places with free access to the internet.

Sell your stuff

You can either hold a garage sale or post your stuff on Craigslist. The money you collect from sales can help you take care of the expenses you need to have covered while you settle into a new situation. Under this circumstance, you must think of creative ways to stay afloat and avoid eating up on your savings account.

Cancel your gym membership

When you had a primary source of income, it would not have mattered if you are still paying for a gym membership that you do not actually use that often. However, at this point, tightening your belt is essential.

Canceling your membership does not mean you will no longer be fit and healthy. There are plenty of other ways to ensure your fitness. You can jog in a nearby park or around your neighborhood. You can still get your much needed cardio workout for free.

Cancel your cable subscription

Lounging on your couch may be a good idea for just a few days, but the once comforting couch can get you stuck to where you are. That is the last thing you want. So, you better cancel your cable subscription to resist the temptation of turning into a couch potato.

Resist the temptation of eating out

When you still had the means, you may have become used to eating out. However, after quitting your job, dining out becomes a luxury. It is an unnecessary expense and it will do nothing but drain your savings when you have other more important things to take care of.

The bottom line is you must keep track of your spending. It is always good to be informed with where you are and where you are leading especially in terms of your finances. Pay attention to your spending and look after your savings.

Have a graceful resignation

Just because you're quitting, it doesn't mean you can tell your bosses to go to hell. Even if it may sound tempting to quit with flair and drama, your sudden outburst can come back to haunt you when it's time to look for a new job.

Remember, all your work experiences go on your record, so it's best to quit and still maintain good terms with your current employer, no matter how badly you've been treated.

Here are the steps you should take to make your exit gracefully:

- Before handing in your resignation, make sure you've finished all tasks previously delegated to you. Don't leave any messes for other people to fix.

- Hand in your resignation with at least two weeks' notice. That way, you are giving your employer enough time to find a replacement.

- When writing your resignation letter, keep the contents brief and to the point. Extensive explanations on a letter might only prove to be a pitfall for you.

- Be factual, but avoid maligning your bosses — those statements can only come back to haunt you, especially since you might need them as character references to your resume.

- You should write only the factors that matter the most, or reasons that are easiest to explain in written form.

- End your resignation letter with a positive note.

- Be prepared to answer your employer's questions, but avoid making accusatory statements. Try to make your exit as positive as you can.

- Clear out your desk and computer before you leave. If you need to turnover some files, keep them organized in a flash drive for your successor.

Making a clean break with your current employer is a great way to start a new career. That way, you will still be assured of a warm welcome when you ever find yourself back in the company's doorstep.

Find a new job before you quit

One of the best backup plan you can ever have is to make sure you already have a job waiting for you immediately after you quit.

After handing out your two weeks notice, you should now spend your time searching for a new job. Or, better yet, you should not hand in that resignation unless you're absolutely sure you can survive the next few weeks without work.

This is especially true if you actually have no savings but still want to resign your current job. It wouldn't be wise on your part to quit if your future is uncertain. You want to minimize your risk as little as possible.

It's okay to take a few days break if you only want to clear your head, but you should be geared to look for new work immediately if your savings are dwindling and you have no other way to pay for the bills.

Conclusion

It's not that easy to leave your current job, particularly if you've had it for years. Most people who seek stability will probably choose to weather it out and hope things pick up in the near future.

However, its crucial to always consider your own emotions and your level of happiness when you are making such an important decision. If there is a lot of obvious signs like depression, anxiety, or just not feeling right about your job, then it might be a good time to think about if you should keep going this career path.

When you've asked yourself the question "Should I quit my job?" several times, it's already an indicator that you should do so. In some situations, quitting is the best decision you could make. You owe it to yourself to make sure you have not only a lucrative job, but a job that you enjoy doing.

Instead of dragging your feet on your way to the exit, prepare for the future and set your priorities straight. Among these preparations include not only writing your resignation letter or fixing loose ends, but also preparing yourself for what you are about to face when you have quit.

When you have fully prepared for it, quitting a job you hate could be the best thing you can do for yourself. With enough time and preparations, you can choose a totally different career path. Just remember, *"You deserve to be happy. Don't let anyone make you forget that!"*

Thank you for reading "Should I Quit My Job?" book, I hope the information in this book can really benefit you to make a better decision on your resignation. If you enjoyed this book, please take some time to share your thoughts and post a review on Amazon. It'd be greatly appreciated.

Thomas.K.Lutz